What do you know of the origin of the universe?

It all began with a Bang!

Have you ever
wondered how the
universe came to be?

How was the
universe created?

You might ask where the stars and the moon come from. Let's go back to where it all started.

Read on and be amazed
by the theories of
how the universe and
everything in it began.

The birth of the universe has been the subject of debates and scientific discussions.

The famous scientists Albert Einstein, Edwin Hubble and Stephen Hawking have tried to uncover the mystery of how the universe developed to become what it is today.

The Big Bang Theory is one of the most famous models of the origin and development of the universe. The Big Bang Theory is an effort to explain about how the universe began: with a huge explosion.

At first there was
nothing, nothing at all.
But after the big burst,
the universe came to be.

The universe started
as a tiny point, a
small singularity.
It was unbelievably
hot and dense.

Suddenly, it exploded and the explosion forced it outward in all directions, and the universe was born.

The Big Bang created the expanding universe as well as time. Before the Big Bang, it was always "now". The universe has expanded over 13.8 billion years to what we know today, and is still expanding.

With the Big Bang, time, space, and matter all began. The universe grows and expands continuously at a fantastic rate.

All of the matter in the universe came into existence from that one tiny singularity. Gravity, the force of attraction, pulled together matter and the first stars and galaxies were born.

As the galaxies expand, they are held together by gravity.

The stars and the galaxies are part of the universe. But there is matter that exists that we can't see.

This is called Dark Matter. We know it exists because we can measure the effects of its gravity. Dark matter comprises 90% of the matter in the universe, according to astronomers.

After the universe began, according to National Aeronautics and Space Administration (NASA), the surrounding temperature was about 10 billion degrees Fahrenheit in the first second.

Vast arrays of fundamental particles were contained in it. These included the neutrons, electrons and protons.

As the universe got cooler, the particles combined. The protons and neutrons combined and formed hydrogen and helium nuclei.

As the universe cooled, atomic nuclei captured electrons from other atoms. The universe was filled with hydrogen and helium gas.

It took a million of
years for the universe
to cool down to the
point where stars
could start to form.

How can the astronomers look back to the universe's birth?

The Big Bang Theory came to be through the mathematical theories and models.

By studying the cosmic microwave background activity, astronomers were able to describe the expansion of the universe.

The universe is still
expanding today. We are
in it. We are among of the
incredible creatures living
in a beautiful planet among
the beautiful stars.

Humans have always been curious about the beginning of the universe. We want to understand about the universe, our home.

The Big Bang Theory gives us an idea of how it all started. The stars in the sky, the planets and their moons, the asteroids and everything in the universe came to be because of the Big Bang!

Made in the USA
Coppell, TX
05 July 2022

WHAT IS THE BIG BANG THEORY AND WHY DOES IT MATTER?

Scientific Kid's Encyclopedia of Space

Cosmology for Kids - Children's Cosmology Books

PROFESSOR GUSTO
EDUCATIONAL & INFORMATIVE BOOKS FOR CHILDREN
(PRE-K / K-12)